Great Canadian Puzzles

Illustrated by
Dominique Pelletier

Scholastic Canada Ltd.
Toronto New York London Auckland Sydney
Mexico City New Delhi Hong Kong Buenos Aires

Scholastic Canada Ltd.
604 King Street West, Toronto, Ontario M5V 1E1, Canada

Scholastic Inc.
557 Broadway, New York, NY 10012, USA

Scholastic Australia Pty Limited
PO Box 579, Gosford, NSW 2250, Australia

Scholastic New Zealand Limited
Private Bag 94407, Greenmount, Auckland, New Zealand

Scholastic Children's Books
Euston House, 24 Eversholt Street, London NW1 1DB, UK

Credits:
pp. 6–7, 10, 11, 15, 24–27, 36, 56, 60, 61, 64, 65: Audrey and Dodie McKim
pp. 12–14, 42–43, 64: Lillian Marcus
pp. 18, 20–21, 48–49: Edith Fowke
pp. 31, 37, 40–41, 46–47, 52–53, 57: Pauline Philip

ISBN-10 0-545-99994-4 / ISBN-13 978-0-545-99994-6

6 5 4 3 2 1 Printed in Canada 07 08 09 10 11

Introduction

Get ready to have some fun! But be careful! You just might learn something about our fantastic country along the way! Answers start on page 72.

Canada

Canada is a vast country that stretches from the Atlantic Ocean to the Pacific Ocean and reaches the Arctic Ocean in the north. The word "Canada" comes from the Iroquois word "kanata," which means village. Canada is famous for its favourite pastime, hockey, as well as its wheat and lakes.

Across

1. Word that "Canada" was taken from
5. Large antlered animal
7. Mountain range shared by B.C. and Alberta
8. Capital of Nova Scotia
10. A white bear
14. A winter vehicle
15. One of three territories
16. Canadian police force (initials)
18. A Great Lake
19. Favourite Canadian pastime
22. New Brunswick capital
23. Famous Prince Edward Island vegetable
24. Aboriginal group

Down

2. Ocean to the north
3. A grain used to make bread
4. Western province (2 words)
6. Long river (2 words)
9. CFL team
11. The Great One
12. Bonhomme's home province
13. French explorer, Jacques ______
17. NHL hockey team (2 words)
20. Delicious fluid from maple tree
21. Canada's capital

1
2
3
4
5
6
7
8
9
10
11
12
13
14
15
16
17
18
19
20
21
22
23
24

Canada

O	N	T	A	R	I	O	Y	D	H	T	N	S	I	O	D	R	W	N	P
D	T	P	X	A	U	F	X	V	I	X	W	A	N	Z	D	H	N	O	R
N	C	I	Z	W	N	E	B	E	F	O	B	S	N	Y	F	I	A	R	I
R	U	F	S	F	J	R	P	C	U	E	A	K	O	C	Y	W	B	T	N
X	R	F	H	B	S	V	R	L	K	B	E	A	V	Z	F	Q	B	H	C
N	W	P	F	D	F	X	Y	C	O	L	D	T	A	P	E	U	R	W	E
A	E	J	N	Y	X	L	D	T	D	N	I	C	S	O	Y	E	I	E	E
B	T	W	P	S	A	H	I	Y	A	G	R	H	C	A	I	B	T	S	D
T	Z	Z	B	I	U	N	W	L	U	U	Z	E	O	D	T	E	I	T	W
V	W	O	Z	R	A	H	D	Y	A	K	E	W	T	O	C	C	S	T	A
F	V	F	O	M	U	N	Y	J	G	B	O	A	I	L	H	K	H	E	R
J	B	Q	Q	X	U	N	H	F	U	A	R	N	A	J	K	S	C	R	D
Y	W	N	A	O	N	C	S	G	W	Q	Y	A	J	I	M	S	O	R	I
C	O	B	F	A	E	U	Q	W	Y	B	L	L	D	S	I	F	L	I	S
D	H	W	R	O	L	W	N	K	I	G	W	B	B	O	D	E	U	T	L
K	E	Y	F	A	W	B	D	A	L	C	B	Y	R	W	R	Z	M	O	A
N	X	F	Y	L	W	X	E	U	V	K	K	C	Y	Q	Q	L	B	R	N
H	A	U	I	D	H	I	N	R	X	U	V	U	O	G	U	S	I	I	D
V	F	Q	G	A	R	C	P	L	T	Z	T	T	S	I	P	X	A	E	C
L	X	Z	G	D	V	Q	I	L	F	A	T	C	Y	F	R	P	N	S	V

Ontario
Manitoba
Saskatchewan
Alberta
British Columbia
Yukon
Northwest Territories
Nunavut
Newfoundland
Labrador
Quebec
Nova Scotia
New Brunswick
Prince Edward Island

Maple Maze

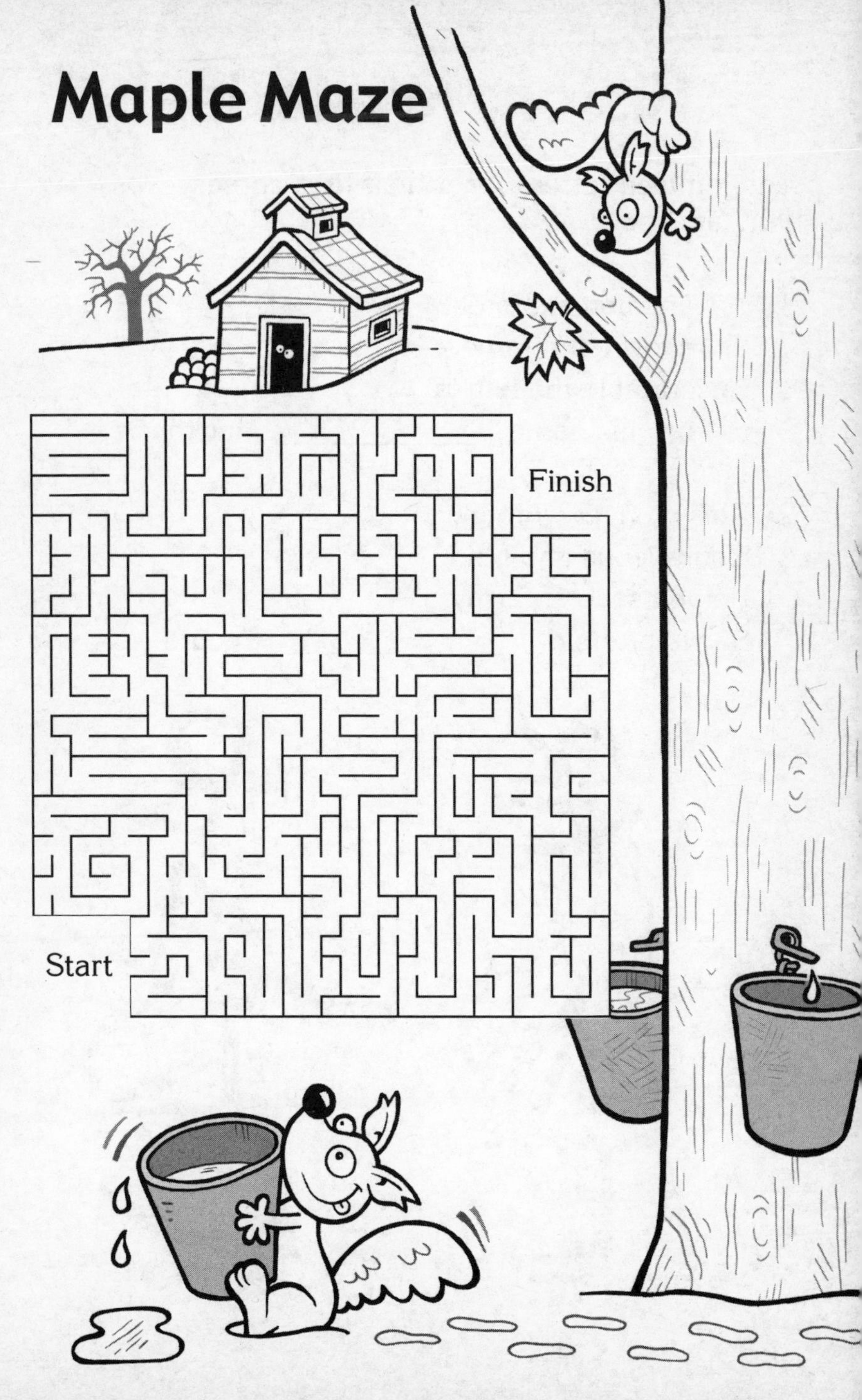

History Mysteries

The jumbled letters form their first names. Who are they?

1. A Canadian explorer
   Of renown and fame —
   Unscramble the letters
   to form his name. ______________ Mackenzie

2. This pioneer woman,
   Courageous and bold,
   Helped save an army
   So we are told. ________________ Secord

3. An early explorer,
His name will not wane;
A native of France, ____________ de Champlain.

4. A famous young nurse
Who came to New France;
Born in 1606,
Her name is ____________________________ Mance.

British Columbia

With the Pacific Ocean to its west, and with the snow-capped peaks of the Rocky Mountains on the east, British Columbia is a dazzling province. Its provincial tree is the western red cedar, and its provincial flower is the Pacific dogwood. British Columbia boasts lots of activities, from skiing, to whale-watching, to walking across the province's longest bridge, the Capilano Suspension Bridge, and enjoying nature.

Across

4. Mythical lake monster
5. Large sea mammals
7. B.C. artist (2 words)
8. One of the sites of the 2010 Winter Olympics
11. Borders this ocean
12. CFL team
14. Grizzly________
15. Provincial flower, Pacific________
18. The __________ Suspension Bridge

Down

1. Port Coquitlam native who ran across Canada (2 words):
2. Province's NHL team
3. Large city
6. Province's neighbour
9. Vancouver's _________ Park
10. Capital city
13. Longest river
16. Native group of B.C.
17. The __________ Mountains

1
2
3
4
5
6
7
8
9
10
11
12
13
14
15
16
17
18

Northern Lights

Fill in the missing letters to discover the names of two important towns in the North.

W My first is in WHITE but not in RED
_____ My second is in SLEIGH but not in SLED
I My third is in MINE and also in MILL
_____ My fourth is in MOUNTAIN but not in HILL
_____ My fifth is in EAST but not in NORTH
H My sixth is in THIRD and also in FOURTH
_____ My seventh is in GOLD but not in TIN
R My eighth is in SNICKER and also in GRIN
_____ My ninth is in SMILE but not in LAUGH
_____ My tenth is in WHOLE but not in HALF
My whole is a city both north and west —
Guess my name and win the test!

Y My first is in CRY but not in WEEP
_____ My second is in RIVER and also in CREEK
L My third is in LAKE but not in SEA
_____ My fourth is in LEAF but not in TREE
O My fifth is in MOOSE but not in DEER
_____ My sixth is in COW but not in STEER
_____ My seventh is in TRACK but not in TRAIL
N My eighth's not in HAMMER but it is in NAIL
_____ My ninth is in SLEIGH but not in SNOW
_____ My tenth is in FLOAT and also in FLOW
E My eleventh is in EASY and also in FREE
My whole is a city in NWT.

What's in a Name?

1. MOOSE JAW, in Saskatchewan, so the legend goes, was named from the fact that a Red River cart was repaired by the jawbone of a moose found on the prairie.

2. The ASSINIBOINE RIVER in Manitoba was named after the Assiniboine people who heated stones to do their cooking.

3. RIDEAU FALLS near Ottawa was named from the French word meaning "curtain."

4. OKOTOKS in Alberta means "many stones" in the Blackfoot language.

5. KELOWNA in the Okanagan Valley in British Columbia means "grizzly bear" in Salish.

6. The KLONDIKE in the Yukon is from another aboriginal word. It means "great river" in Gwich'in.

7. FLIN FLON, a mining town in Manitoba, was named after a character in a book that some prospectors were reading called *The Sunless City* by J.E. Preston-Muddock. Who was the character? Professor Flintabbatey Flonatin!

8. ALBERTA was named for Queen Victoria's husband, Prince Albert.

Secret Codes

Use the chart below to decode these words.

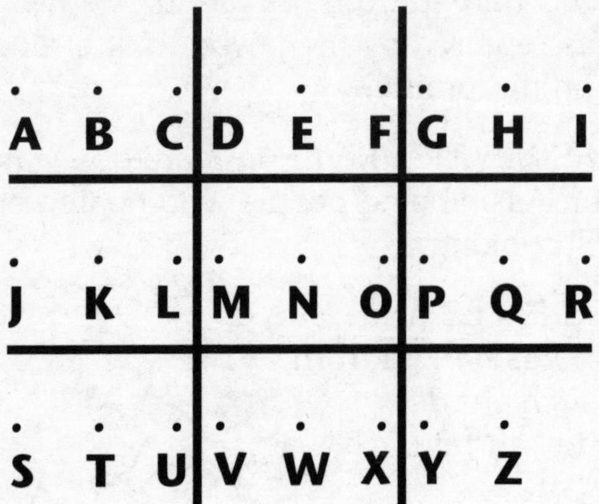

Example: G O L F

Secret Codes

Sports

1 ____

2 ____

3 ____

4 ____

5 ____

Secret Codes

Languages

1 ____________________

2 ____________________

3 ____________________

4 ____________________

Canadian Riddles

1. Why can't a man living in Halifax be buried west of the Red River?
2. What Canadian animals are found in banks?
3. How far can a dog run into the northern woods?
4. Is it legal for a man in Saskatchewan to marry his widow's sister?
5. A Canadian builds a house rectangular in shape. Each side has a southern exposure. A big bear comes wandering by the house. What colour is the bear?

Alberta

Alberta is bordered by the Rocky Mountains to the west and Saskatchewan to the east. Calgary is home to the annual Calgary Stampede. The province has rich oil fields and is famous for its Dinosaur Provincial Park, located in the Alberta Badlands.

Across

3. Largest of Canada's Rocky Mountain Parks
6. ____________ Provincial Park
7. Natural resource
8. The Calgary ____________
9. Warm wind that blows in off the Rockies
10. An aboriginal group of Alberta
12. The beef capital of Canada
14. Biggest lake
15. Inland bodies of water
18. Edmonton's hockey stars

Down

1. Capital city
2. Location of Dinosaur Provincial Park, the ____________
4. Neighbouring province
5. Red, fragrant flower
11. Calgary's NHL team
13. A grain
16. Winter sport
17. Animals found in the woods

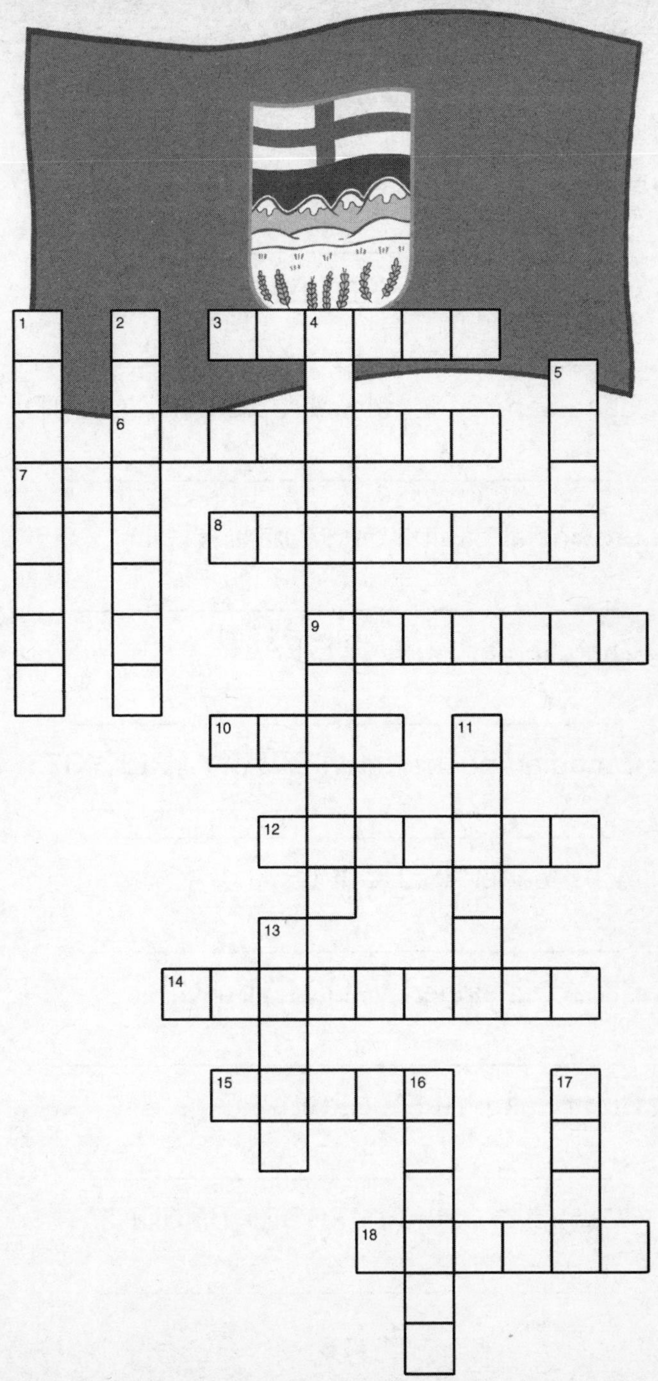
1
2
3
4
5
6
7
8
9
10
11
12
13
14
15
16
17
18

Scrambled Names

1. A Canadian explorer: DNAAEEXRL EEMNKIACZ

____

2. A marathon runner: RETRY OXF

____

3. A Canadian prime minister: EERPIR UURATDE

____

4. A provincial capital city: OMNENTOD

____

5. A Canadian artist: LMYIE RACR

____

6. A Canadian hockey star: EWANY TREKYGZ

____

7. A Métis leader: ISLUO IRLE

____

8. A Canadian singer: VALIR EVIANGL

____

9. A Great Lake: ALKE URSEIPRO

____

10. A Canadian author: RRBOET HMUCNS

____

Start

Finish

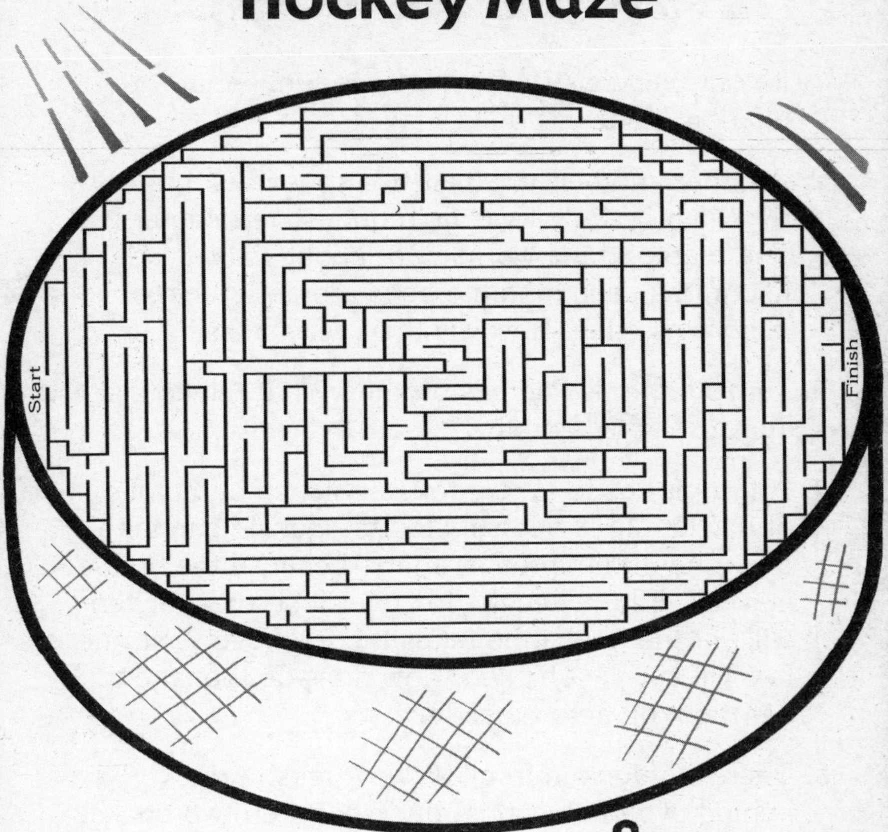

How's Your Logic?

1. If your uncle's sister is not your aunt, what relation is she to you?
2. A father, mother and their two sons must cross a river in a boat that will hold only sixty kilograms. The man and the woman are about sixty kilograms each, and the boys are about thirty kilograms each. How will they get across?
3. Tom's father is Paddy's brother. What relation is Tom to Paddy's mother?
4. A farmer has to take a fox, a chicken and a bag of chicken feed across a footbridge. He can take only one of the three at a time because the bridge is weak. If he takes the fox over first, the chicken will eat the feed. If he takes the feed over first, the fox will eat the chicken. How does he manage to get them all across safely?
5. There's a duck in front of two ducks, a duck behind two ducks and a duck between two ducks. How many ducks are there all together?
6. Two men are walking down the street and a girl passes them. One of the men stops to speak to the girl. The other man says, "You must know that girl." "Yes," the first replies, "that girl's father was my father's only son." What relation is the girl to the man?

7. Two mothers and two daughters go shopping, and they each buy a dress, but when they all bring them home they only have three dresses. How can this be?

8. You must choose between two doors, one leading to life and the other to death. There are two men in the room: one always tells the truth and the other always lies. You are allowed to ask only one question. How can you find which door leads to life?

9. A teacher wants to find the cleverest student to represent the school in a television quiz. When the choice is narrowed down to three — Thomas, Jane and Winnie — the teacher blindfolds them and tells them he is putting either a red maple leaf or a blue maple leaf on each of their foreheads. They are then to take off the blindfolds, and if they see a blue maple leaf on any forehead, they are to raise their hands. The first to figure out the colour of the maple leaf on his or her forehead will be the winner. The teacher then puts a blue maple leaf on all three foreheads. Naturally, all three raise their hands, which doesn't tell anyone what colour is on their foreheads. A short time later Jane solves the mystery. How?

Saskatchewan

Saskatchewan is bordered by the Northwest Territories to the north, Alberta to the west and Manitoba to the east. Its provincial tree is the white birch. The white-tailed deer is common in northern parts of the province. In 2001 the province made curling its official sport. Saskatchewan is also home to the Royal Canadian Mounted Police training academy, located in Regina. The province's principal industries are agriculture, mining, manufacturing and tourism. And the town of Estevan is the country's sunshine capital.

Across

3. Where to find Mounties-in-training
4. Small prairie animal
7. The white-tailed ________
8. Saskatchewan's official sport
10. A grain
11. River in Saskatchewan
12. Important provincial industry
13. Aboriginal native of Saskatchewan
14. These large animals used to roam the plains
15. Something used in curling
16. Canada's sunshine capital

Down

1. Saskatchewan's territorial neighbour (2 words)
2. Place to store grain
5. Provincial football team
6. Provincial tree, white ________
9. Former premier and "Greatest Canadian"_______ Douglas

1
2
3
4
5
6
7
8
9
10
11
12
13
14
15
16

Riddle, Riddle!

1. When is a train like water?
2. When are men and women of the RCMP like oranges?
3. What is the strongest bird in Canada?
4. When is our weather like a king?
5. What Canadian cup has no handles?
6. Every child in Canada spends much time making it, yet no one can see it. What is it?
7. How do you know Peace River is rich?
8. Why do people swim in Lake Ontario?

A Canadian City

Can you find the missing letters?

S My first is in SILVER but not in GOLD
_____ My second's in TELL and also in TOLD
_____ My third is in JANE and also in JILL
O My fourth is in MOUNTAIN but not in HILL
_____ My fifth's in HOTEL but not in INN
_____ My sixth is in NECK and also in CHIN
S My seventh's in HARVEST but not in REAP
My whole is a city whose harbour is deep.

Beware! Wild animals!

A wild animal of Canada is hidden in each of the following sentences. Can you spot them?

1. John, please be a very careful driver.
2. You must only go at the rate of forty kilometres per hour.
3. Those people may be ardent photographers.
4. In the test, Bill's side erased all the answers.
5. In the field, a cow's moo sent birds flying.
6. The overheated tunnel kindled a flame.
7. Don't ask unkempt boys to wash dishes.
8. Suresh is not terrific as a guitar player.
9. Put the Jello on the dessert plate.
10. I knew him in kindergarten.
11. Did you use all the shampoo?

O Canada!

Unscramble the words to find out what this building means to Canadians.

The tower is called the ________ Tower. (EAPCE)
The building is in the city of ________. (TOTOAW)
It is one of a collection of massive buildings forming a great ________. (QSUREA)
Here people assemble for important Canadian ________. (STEVEN)
It is the ________ of (TEAS)
the ________ (LEEFRAD)
government of
Canada.

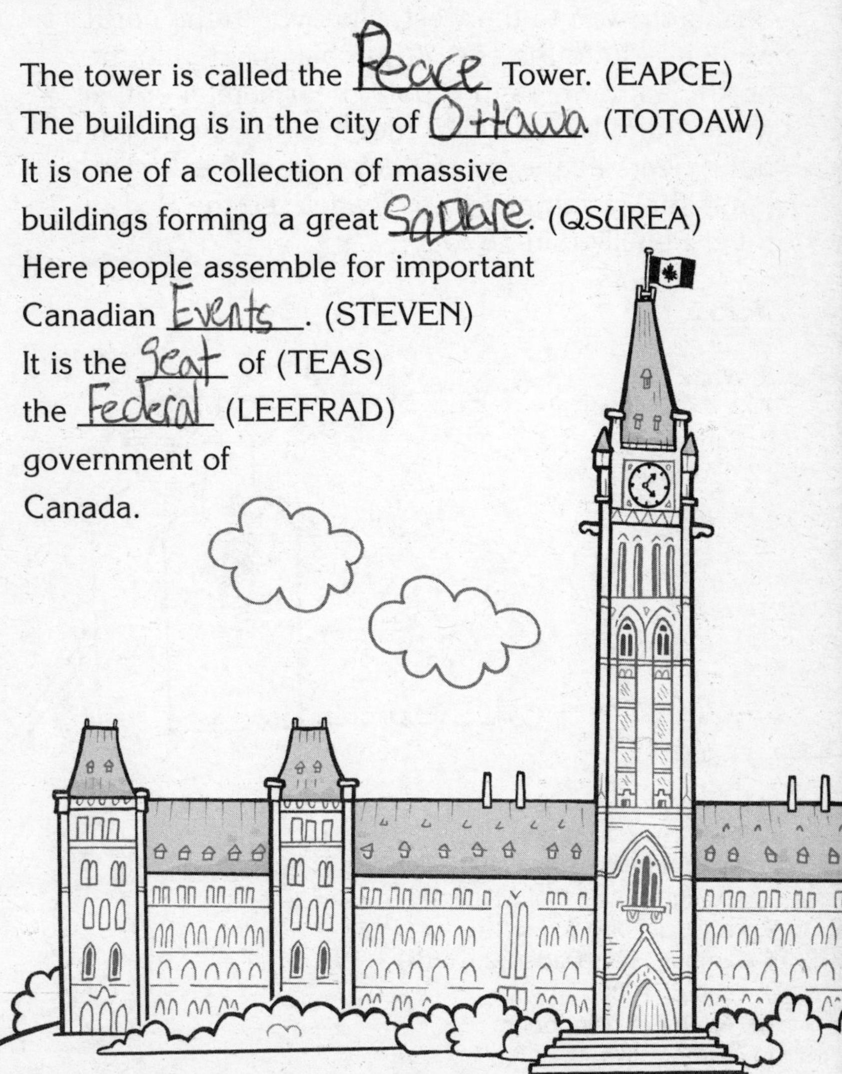

Manitoba

Rich with forests and lakes, Manitoba is known as the "Land of 1000 Lakes." It is bordered by Saskatchewan to the west, Nunavut to the north and Ontario to the east. Churchill, located in the north, is known as the "polar bear capital of the world," and in the winter months you can watch polar bears as they come down from the Arctic. Louis Riel, a famous Métis leader, led the Red River Rebellion in 1870.

Across

2. The ______ Bay
5. White bear
7. Polar bear capital
9. Capital city
12. Provincial flower

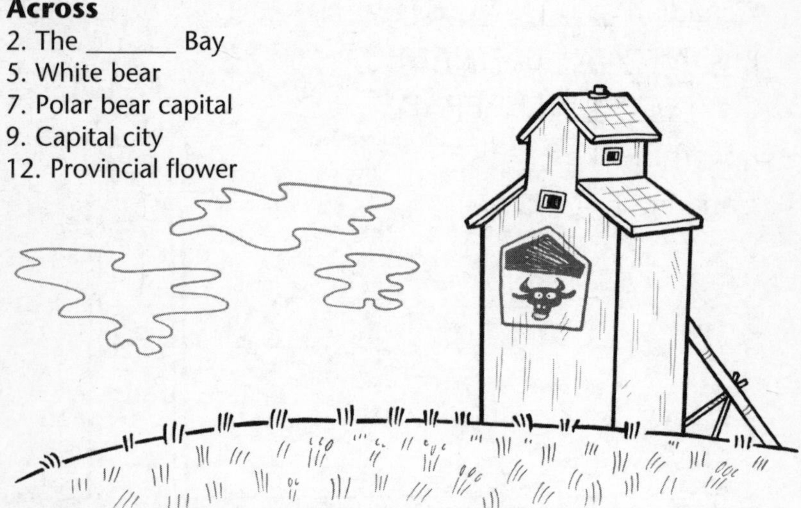

Down

1. Famous bear named after Winnipeg (3 words)
3. Aboriginal native of Manitoba
4. Provincial bird (2 words)
6. Famous Métis leader (2 words)
8. Land of 1000 ____
10. Northern neighbour
11. Famous fort

1
2
3
4
5
6
7
8
9
10
11
12

Moose Crossing Maze

Find the correct path through the maze.

Jumbled Jobs

Unscramble the letters below to find jobs.

1. TISTDNE ______________________
2. RIETRW ______________________
3. AIUSCMIN ______________________
4. ITSCTEINS ______________________
5. ERKNAB ______________________
6. ROTCA ______________________
7. RHCETEA ______________________
8. NVENRAIATERI ______________________
9. RENSU ______________________
10. RNADCE ______________________
11. ROOGPHTHEPAR ______________________
12. GDUJE ______________________
13. RTSIAT ______________________
14. DROCTO ______________________
15. BREMPLU ______________________
16. ERORTREP ______________________
17. AHSPMRTCIA ______________________
18. NLIARAIRB ______________________

Hockey Puzzle

T Q F C R W K D V S Q H P P

P K Z S F K H T P K T T J U

A B T F C M O Y Y A G A V G

D D D Z Y J C B C T L P Y E

S R A T M T K Z H E O R S H

Z O H V A A E Z S S V C E H

G B G F Z V Y N S Z E C R J

T Y Z O G S E B B X S E L X

C U S U A F B D R H X N R J

W G Q S E L C D W T R T U K

U W L D J Q I Y S V Q R E N

F E Q M A L J E L E A E T O

Hockey
Skates
Gloves
Pads
Goalie
Defense
Centre

Countries

Unscramble the letters to find the countries from which people travel to Canada.

1. ENUIDT AESTST ______________________
2. DUINET IKNMODG ______________________
3. ANPJA ______________________
4. FAENRC ______________________
5. EMRNYAG ______________________
6. EIOMCX ______________________
7. ASIARALUT ______________________
8. USOHT OKAER ______________________
9. ENHREANTDSL ______________________
10. AICNH ______________________
11. OGNH OKGN ______________________
12. WTNAAI ______________________
13. ESWIZLNARDT ______________________
14. DNIAI ______________________
15. LIYAT ______________________

Ontario

Ontario is home to numerous lakes, large mineral resources like nickel, and abundant forests. It also contains rich farmland and one third of the population of Canada. There are lots of fun things to do like hiking, skiing, snowmobiling, fishing or swimming. Toronto, its capital city, has the world's tallest structure, the CN Tower, and is home to the Toronto Maple Leafs.

Across

1. Ottawa NHL team
3. Toronto NHL team (2 words)
5. Government home
6. World's largest freshwater lake (2 words)
10. The Hudson ___________
11. Location of the Big Nickel
12. The Great _______
14. Aboriginal group of Ontario
15. A winter vehicle

Down

2. Waterfall city (2 words)
4. The CN ___________
7. Capital city of Canada
8. Neighbouring province
9. Provincial capital
13. A group of trees

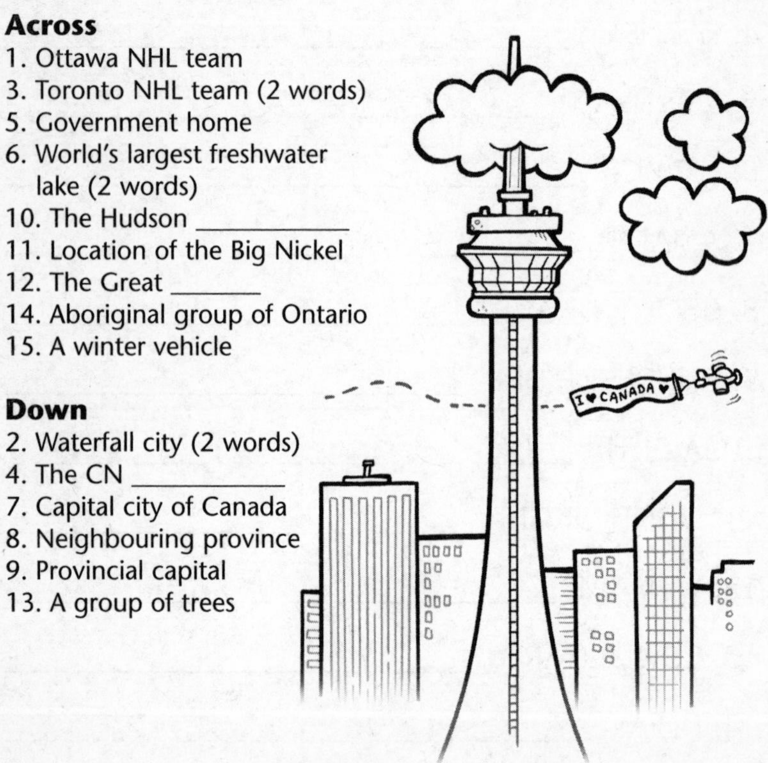

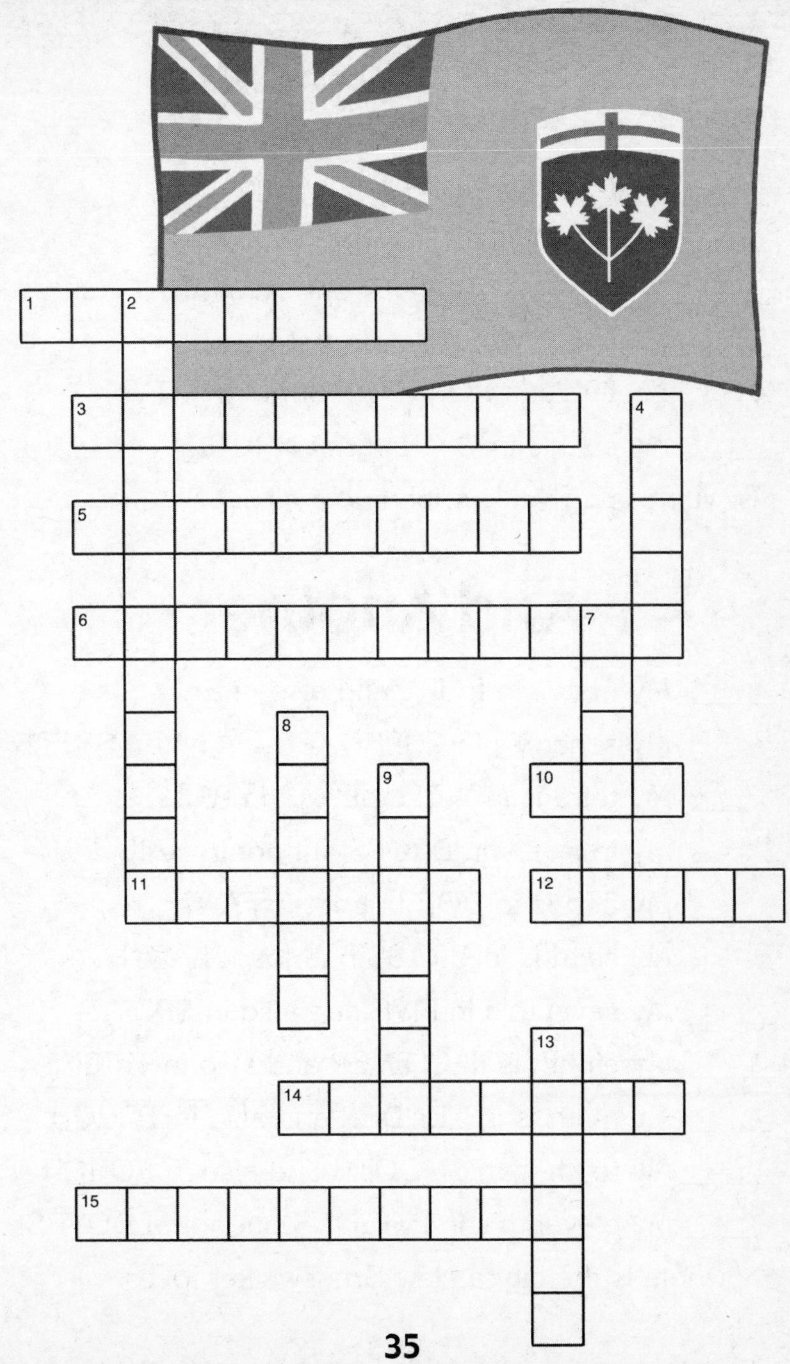

1
2
3
4
5
6
7
8
9
10
11
12
13
14
15

Riddle-a-City!

O My first letter's in DOG but not in PUP
______ My second's in TEA but not in CUP
______ My third's in TOPPER but also in HAT
______ My fourth's in OVAL but also in FLAT
W My fifth's in SORROW but not in PITY
______ My sixth's in CAT but not in KITTY
My whole is a river, a tribe and a city.

And Another

______ My first is in FAIRY and also in ELF
R My second's in CUPBOARD but not in SHELF
______ My third is in WELL but not in PAIL
D My fourth is in DROPS but not in HAIL
______ My fifth is in DOE but not in FAWN
R My sixth is in GRASS but not in LAWN
______ My seventh's in FIVE and also in SIX
______ My eighth is in CLEVER and also in TRICKS
______ My ninth is in TENDER and also in TOUGH
______ My tenth is in SMOOTH and also in ROUGH
______ My eleventh's in PIGEONS but not in DOVES
My whole is the city a New Brunswicker loves.

Canadian Weather

Unscramble the letters below to find some weather words.

1. ANRI ______________________
2. ELTSE ______________________
3. DOORATN ______________________
4. ITMS ______________________
5. TRSFO ______________________
6. DCOYUL ______________________
7. ECRHIRNUA ______________________
8. IHLA ______________________
9. GHLNGTIIN ______________________
10. WSON ______________________
11. LRZADZBI ______________________
12. DINW ______________________
13. GOF ______________________
14. ENHDUTR ______________________
15. CIE ______________________

Quebec

Quebec is Canada's largest province and has lots to do, like whale-watching in the St. Lawrence River or taking to the slopes to ski. It's Canada's main exporter of maple syrup and is famous for its winter festival, Carnaval, hosted by that happy snowman, Bonhomme. The most famous winter vehicle, the snowmobile, was invented in Quebec by Joseph-Armand Bombardier. Quebec is also home to the Canadian Space Agency, which has sent astronauts like Marc Garneau, Julie Payette and Roberta Bondar into space.

Across

4. The St. _______________ River
5. Common language spoken in Quebec
8. The __________ Canadiens
9. Delicious Quebec export (2 words)
11. Explorer Jacques __________
12. St. Lawrence residents
14. Inventor of the snowmobile, Joseph-Armand _______________

Down

1. French for *thank you*
2. Capital city
3. Canada's first astronaut (2 words)
6. Famous snowman
7. Winter festival
10. A structure used to provide energy
13. Winter sport

Wagon Wheel

See how many words you can make by starting at any letter and following the paths to the other letters. You can use a letter more than once in a word, but you have to follow the paths.

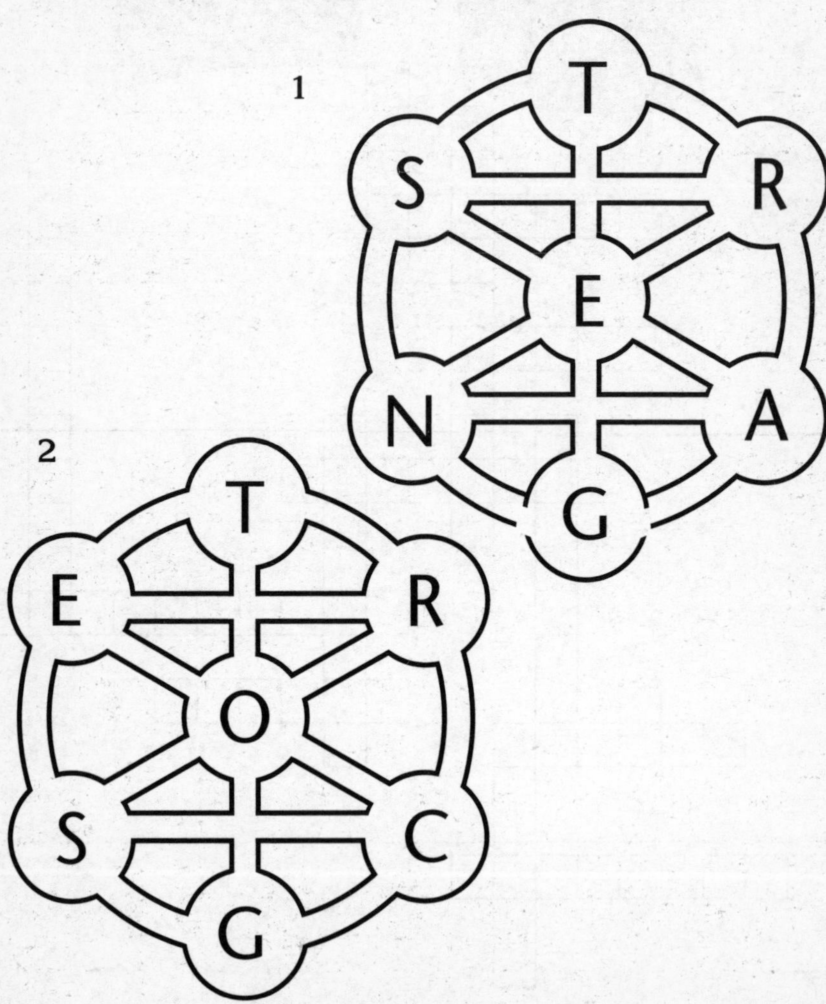

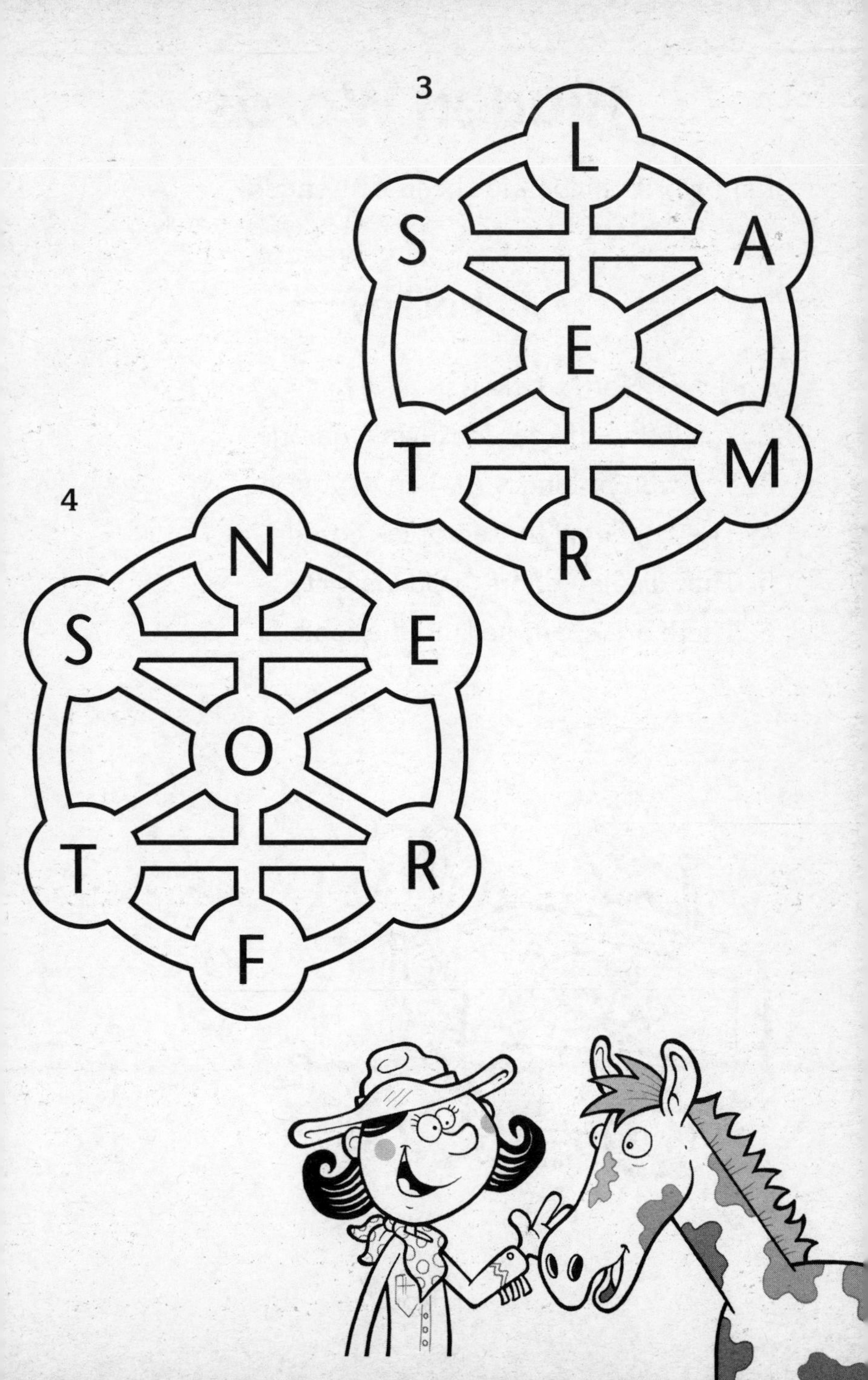
3
L
S
A
E
T
M
R
4
N
S
E
O
T
R
F

Hidden Words

Find words hidden in these sentences.

Hockey

1. Here's Mom's ticket.
2. You'll find the car in Kevin's garage.
3. You won at bingo, Al. I envy you.
4. They need all those apples cored.
5. That display offers good visibility.
6. There are spare nails in the toolbox.

Winter

1. It's no wonder you have a bad cold.
2. Is Lee taking a holiday this year?
3. The notice says that the music ends at midnight.
4. Is Eric older than Akiko?
5. Watch that pendulum as it moves to and fro steadily.
6. There must be free zebras somewhere in the world.

Breakfast Foods

1. This meat sauce really tastes good.
2. This clothes peg got wet.
3. Let's decide which one yodels the loudest.
4. We can't all go into a store for just one item.
5. Who gave Rob a concert ticket for his birthday?
6. Emil kept his promise to babysit last night.
7. Nivetha wore striped pyjamas last night.

New Brunswick

New Brunswick is one of Canada's three Maritime provinces. The Bay of Fundy, located between New Brunswick and Nova Scotia, is known for having the highest tides in the world. When Samuel de Champlain began exploring the province in the 1600s, he met the Mi'kmaq and Maliseet peoples who lived there. New Brunswick is Canada's only official bilingual province. The province is known for its fishing, including its delicious lobster.

Across

2. New Brunswick is one of three _____ Provinces
4. Popular industry
6. Provincial bird, the black-capped ______
7. Aboriginal group
8. Bridge linking New Brunswick to PEI
9. Major city
10. Mountain range

Down

1. Explorer Samuel de ____________
3. One of the official languages of New Brunswick
4. Capital city
5. Provincial neighbour (2 words)

Crack the Code

Cities of the World

Decode the name of each city.

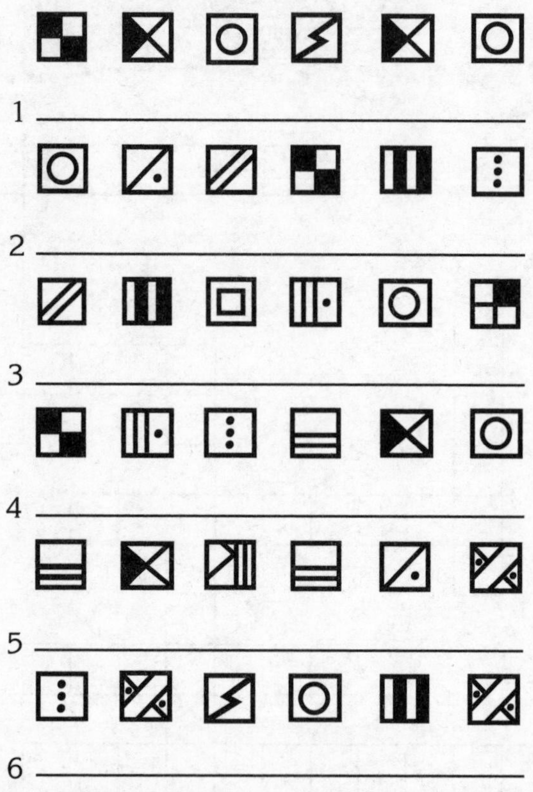

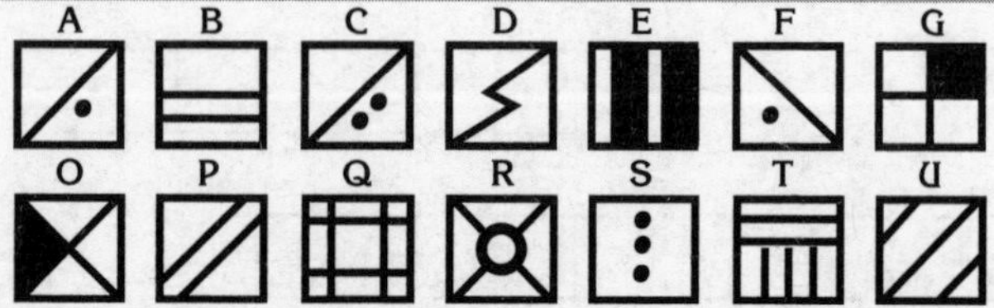

Countries of the World

Now, decode some countries.

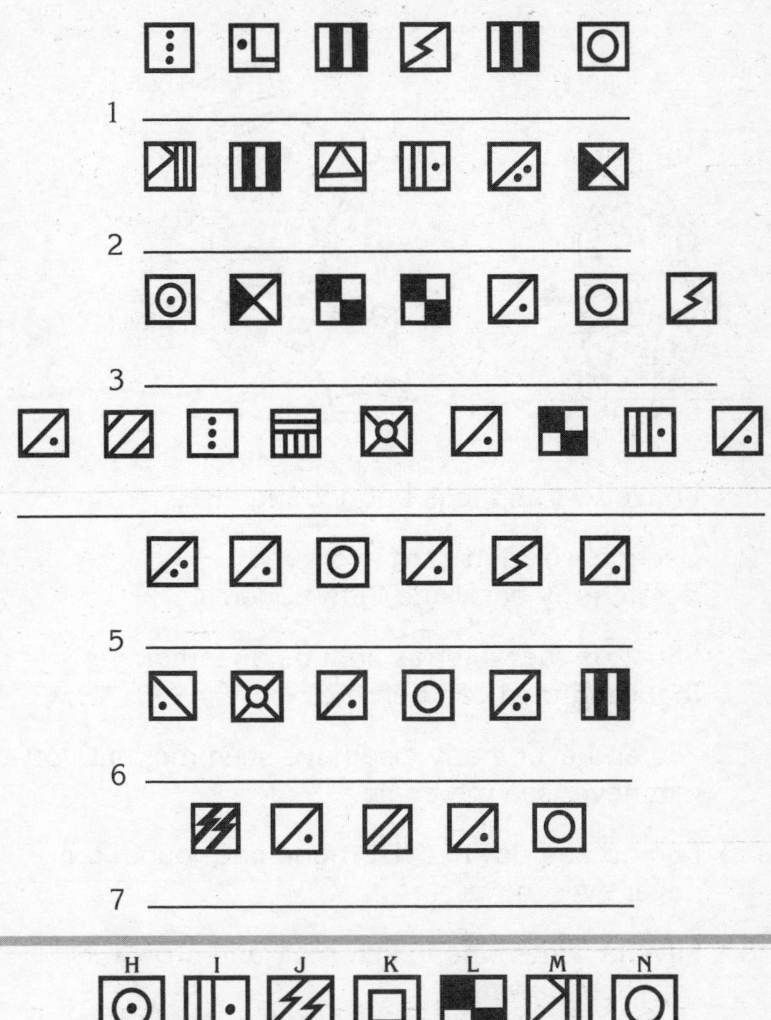

H I J K L M N

V W X Y Z

Guess My Name

1. I have feet and legs but nothing else.
2. Use me well and I am everybody.
   Scratch my back and I am nobody.
3. I float on the water as light as a feather, yet a thousand men can't lift me.
4. You and everybody else have seen me, but you can never see me again.
5. I go up and down, twist round and round, but never ever move.
6. I live in winter, die in summer, and grow with my roots upwards.
7. If you feed me I will live, but if you give me water I die.

8. I am neither in the house nor out of the house, but I still am part of the house.

9. I run all the way from Toronto to Vancouver, but never move.

10. I am nothing but holes tied to holes, yet I am as strong as steel.

11. If my name is spoken, I am broken.

12. I am too much for one, just right for two, but nothing at all for three.

13. I am filled every morning and emptied every night, except once a year when I am filled at night and emptied in the morning.

14. I have a bank but no money; I have branches but no leaves.

15. I stand on one foot and have my heart in my head.

Prince Edward Island

Prince Edward Island is Canada's smallest province and is sometimes referred to as "The Garden Island." *Anne of Green Gables*, by Lucy Maud Montgomery, was set on PEI, and has made the island popular amongst tourists. The Charlottetown Conference, where leaders from across British North America discussed Canadian confederation, lead to the British North American Act in 1867. The province is also known for its potatoes and lobster.

Across

4. Capital city
6. The Act passed in 1867 (initials)
7. Aboriginal group
9. Famous PEI export
10. Provincial short form

Down

1. *Anne of* _____ ______ (2 words)
2. Longest bridge in Canada, the _____ Bridge
3. Prince Edward Island is also known as the ____ _____ (2 words)
5. Delicious crustacean
8. Lucy Maud ____________

1
2
3
4
5
6
7
8
9
10

Hidden Words

How many small words can you find in the words listed here?

Leprechauns

Archeologist

Sportsmanship

Ornithologist

Personality

Valentines

Christmas

Destination

Fireplace

Nova Scotia

Nova Scotia is the second-smallest province in Canada. Its name means "New Scotland." The province is known for its highland dancing and fiddle music, and is famous for the *Bluenose*, which is found on the back of the ten-cent coin. Sable Island, a small island off the coast of Nova Scotia, is well-known for its wild horses.

Across

3. Nova Scotia borders this ocean
4. Traditional Scottish skirt
5. Schooner featured on the back of the ten-cent coin
10. Explorer Samuel ___________
12. Location of wild horses (2 words)
13. Bay with the highest tides in the world

Down

1. Type of dancing popular in Nova Scotia
2. These people were expelled from Nova Scotia in 1755
6. Beacons of light found on the coast
7. Large Nova Scotian island (2 words)
8. Nova Scotia means this: New___________
9. Type of instrument popular in Nova Scotia
11. Capital city

Queenly Cities

Can you fill in the missing letters?

______ My first is in RIVER and also in CREEK
______ My second's in LIVER and also in LEEK
G My third is in GREEN and also in GREEK
______ My fourth is in WINK but not in PEEK
______ My fifth is in PINE but not in TEAK
______ My sixth is in BRAVE but not in MEEK
My whole is a city whose name is unique!

______ My first is in CANVAS but not in TENT
I My second's in FASTING but not in LENT
______ My third is in COOKIE and also in CAKE
______ My fourth is in STREAM but not in LAKE
______ My fifth is in LOVE but not in LIKE
R My sixth is in RUBBER but not in BIKE
______ My seventh's in PINK but not in GREEN
______ My eighth is in FAT and also in LEAN

My whole is a city that's named for a Queen.

Happy Holidays

Unscramble the letters below to find holiday words.

1. ASDLECN ______________________________
2. OMY PPUKRI ______________________________
3. SNOTIEDORAC ______________________________
4. ZAANWAK ______________________________
5. WEN ERYA ______________________________
6. RCIHTSAMS ______________________________
7. EERSTA ______________________________
8. USCIM ______________________________
9. WDLIAI ______________________________
10. EPETSRSN ______________________________
11. MDRAANA ______________________________
12. KTASINHNGIVG ______________________________
13. FODO ______________________________
14. DACRS ______________________________
15. RPSVAOSE ______________________________
16. AEJN-PTBSAITE ______________________________
17. NDCNAGI ______________________________
18. RPYASER ______________________________

Newfoundland and Labrador

With its breathtaking view of the Atlantic Ocean where icebergs can be seen floating by in late spring, Newfoundland and Labrador is Canada's most eastern province. Labrador, on mainland Canada, is separated from the island of Newfoundland by the Strait of Belle Isle. The province boasts the richest area for fish in the world, the Grand Banks, where cod can be found. L'Anse aux Meadows is one of the oldest settlements in the country, where the Vikings visited over 9000 years ago.

Across

4. Important provincial industry
6. Richest area of fish in the world (2 words)
9. The part of the province on mainland Canada
13. Historical Viking settlement (3 words)
14. Frequently seen floating in the ocean

Down

1. The ________ Ocean
2. First foreigners to settle in Canada?
3. Aboriginal group
5. Strait of _________ (2 words)
7. Capital city (2 words)
8. City in Newfoundland
10. Province that borders Labrador
11. Fur-bearing sea animal
12. Famous type of fish

1
2
3
4
5
6
7
8
9
10
11
12
13
14

The Legend of Qu'Appelle Valley

One evening, long, long ago, a young Aboriginal man travelling to his wedding heard his name called out. It was the voice of his sweetheart, but she, he knew, was many days away in camp. Puzzled, the young man answered, "Who calls?" (*Qu'appelle*, in French). The only response was a spirit voice mimicking his question: "Who calls?" Troubled, the boy sped homeward, only to learn that his loved one had died. With her last breath she had called his name.

Ever since, so this legend goes, the valley has been known as the "Qu'appelle" or "Calling River" valley. Some, however, claim the name comes simply from the marvellous echo which rebounds from the valley's walls.

Who knows?

The Qu'Appelle Valley is in Saskatchewan, one of the province's most beautiful and richest river valleys.

About Prime Ministers

Did you know that

– Sir Robert Borden rode a bicycle to Parliament?

– Sir John Abbott was the first prime minister to be born in Canada?

– Louis St. Laurent spoke to his mother in English and his father in French?

– Sir Charles Tupper lived the longest? (until his 95th year)

– John Diefenbaker sold newspapers as a boy?

– Lester B. Pearson's wife used to ask him not to forget the hamburger on his way home from work?

– When Pierre Trudeau first appeared in Parliament, as a member from Quebec, he was scolded by Prime Minister John Diefenbaker for wearing sandals and casual clothes?

The First!

Born in Scotland, an immigrant to Canada, he helped build a nation.

Here are the vowels of his first and last names:

A O A O

Here are the consonants:

M C J D N L N D H

Who was he?

Yukon

Many types of wildlife such as caribou, grizzly bears and peregrine falcons make their home in the Yukon territory. Silver, gold, diamonds and other minerals are mined in the territory. Yukon is home to many Aboriginal groups, including the Tlingit and the Gwich'in First Nations. The territory's official bird is the raven, and its official tree is the sub-alpine fir.

Across

2. Yukon's official bird
6. Province bordering Yukon (2 words)
7. Yukon ______ Rush
8. __________ Lake
10. Capital city
11. Large white bear found in the north

Down

1. Type of bear found in Yukon
3. Aboriginal group
4. Official territorial tree (2 words)
5. Peregrine _______
9. Aurora _______

1
2
3
4
5
6
7
8
9
10
11

Hidden Words

Try to find the hidden words in these sentences.

Numbers

1. When I'm ill I only need to rest to get well.
2. There were four teenagers at the party on Saturday.
3. This event you are describing sounds very interesting.
4. There's an old fort you should visit if you have time.
5. That's quite a weight you are carrying.
6. Bill, I only need your help for a moment.

Front and Back

To find the name of this big inland port, add the same pair of letters to the front and the back of the letters given below:

_ _ RON _ _

Newfoundland Riddle

Name the place: From the word "Nose"
Take the tip away,
Then add it to "Go"
And discover a Bay.

Quick 'n Easy

Fill in the missing letters and you will have the name of a large eastern river.

A _ K	to question
S _ Y	a place for pigs
F _ Y	a small insect
R _ T	a small animal
O _ E	to be in debt
O _ E	a mineral deposit
T _ N	a number
O _ E	another number
A _ T	to play a part
F _ W	not many

Nunavut

Nunavut is Canada's newest territory. "Nunavut" means "our land" in the Inuit language of Inuktitut. Its capital city is Iqaluit and is located on the territory's largest island, Baffin Island. Wild animals like seals, polar bears and caribou can be found across the vast northern territory.

Across

1. Nunavut borders this body of water (2 words)
4. Meaning of "Nunavut" (2 words)
6. A province Nunavut borders
8. Capital city
9. Animal common to Nunavut
11. Large territorial island
12. An Inuit language
13. Ice commonly found in the Arctic

Down

2. Transportation vehicle common in the north
3. Type of bear common to territory
5. Aboriginal people of Nunavut
7. Symbol on flag
9. Type of Inuit art
10. Nunavut borders this ocean

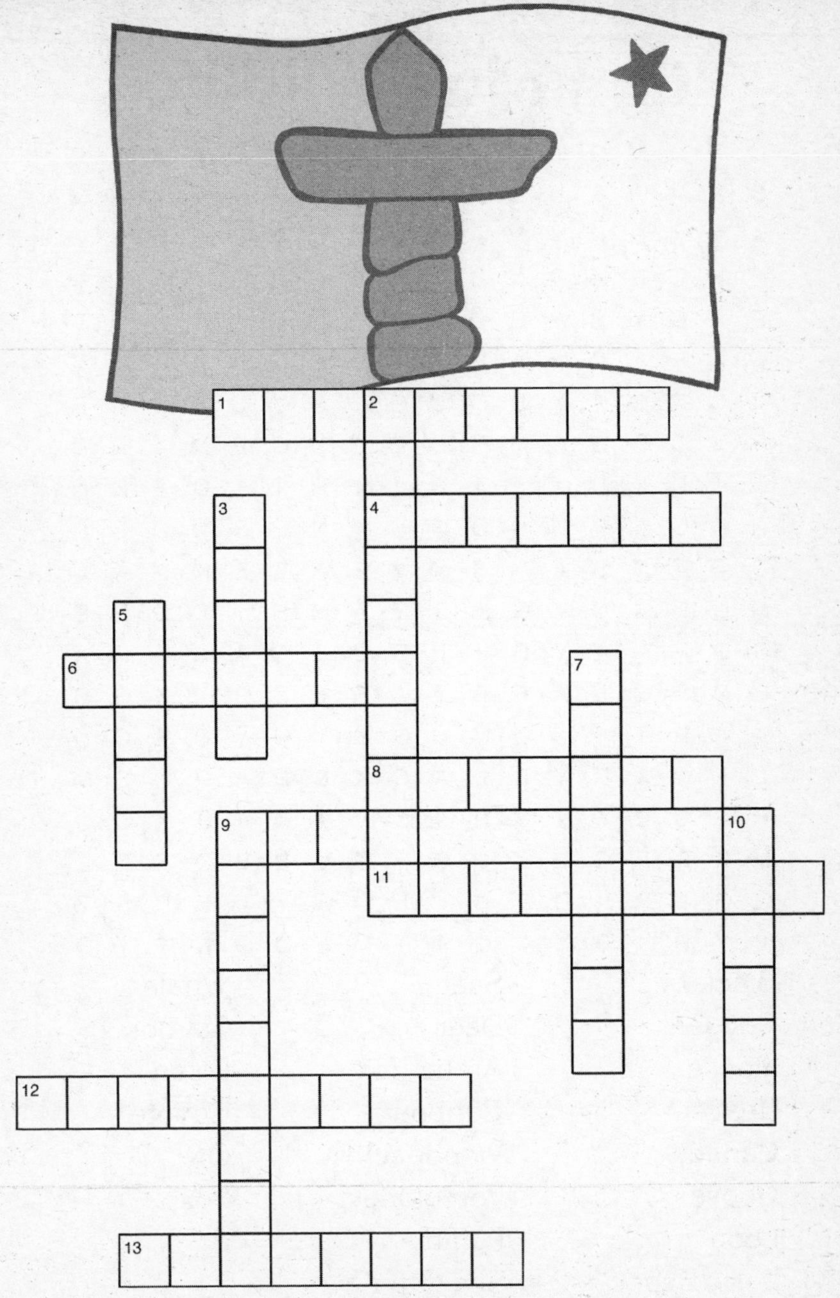
1
2
3
4
5
6
7
8
9
10
11
12
13

Canada's Wildlife

Q U G M G W P Y B A K X B E A V E R
G N V W B U R X D K B Z P M Y J R M
A F X H P Y P A W M D L V D R B H G
F R E R K O N U E W E U H E A X W S
C J C Y H A R D F S Q D C E S H O V
S X K T C M A C O F U R O R A W O Z
Z C C O I X B O U O I S Y C L B D E
P V O C W C M S B P H N O P M I P D
G I U S U T F I B J I R T I O S E N
R D G L P U R O G H Y N E S N O C S
C F A S S A M S X V G W E E M N K C
M G R E C V G M I Y A M H I C D E B
S G P A I Y B I L S B J C A H P R X
E O P O L A R B E A R F Z G L X G R
A W R T A Z O M U G B Y Q Y O E C U
L L Q T B Y B L A C K B E A R O S M
R B C E F Z Z N J X V T I J J X S O
M K P R G L Z U D H S M D V O Z D E
Q G L P K D T B L L O W Y F Y D S Z
V Y H J P X L Q J T M L O O N T Y Q

Black bear
Cougar
Moose
Beaver
Canada
Goose
Loon
Polar Bear

Seal
Deer
Arctic Fox
Caribou
Woodpecker
Porcupine
Puffin
Sea Otter

Whale
Salmon
Bison
Coyote
Owl
Fox

Canadian Landmarks

L K E N E S C T N L V Z R Y H C M S
Q N H W H I O T V X C K X N M V C V
Z P L U L F N T B G N L S X G M H T
F A Q G D D F Z N U T N D R C A A J
J R G A W S E C P Q O R R B V W T M
Y L N S G Y D A J G W R G E P B E Q
S I I A G R E N V R E E B D R A A I
G A A D R C R A D E R X A B U N U T
S M G D A A A D P A T Z Y E J F F K
B E A L N H T I O T J L O C A F R D
W N R E D B I A J L O C F Y K H O O
H T A D B A O N B A Q X F V X O N V
V P F O A A N S U K G W U U U T T T
R G A M N B B H I E Y O N Y K E E Z
O S L E K P R I B S M H D R T L N K
C V L D S N I E M Z I C Y D W R A C
K R S I N R D L I C C U W K Y J C A
I V R B O I G D M B A D L A N D S W
E B W E S T E D M O N T O N M A L L
S G M R Q I N E L Q E C R Z L Y F A

CN Tower
Saddledome
Badlands
Confederation Bridge
Parliament
Banff Hotel
West Edmonton Mall
Chateau Frontenac
Rockies
Bay of Fundy
Canadian Shield
Great Lakes
Grand Banks
Niagara Falls

Northwest Territories

The Northwest Territories is one of Canada's three territories. Its capital city, Yellowknife, is located on the north shore of Great Slave Lake. Many wild animals can be found in the territory, including polar bears, caribou and beluga whales. Its territorial tree is the tamarack, and its territorial bird is the gyr falcon. The territory's official gemstone is the diamond. The Northwest Territories is also known for its beautiful display of the aurora borealis, or Northern Lights.

Across

2. Type of whale found in the NWT
5. Capital city
8. A province that borders NWT
9. Territorial gem
11. Territorial tree

Down

1. Aurora borealis (2 words)
2. Polar ______
3. Mineral mined in the NWT
4. A territory that borders the NWT
6. Four-legged animal found in the NWT
7. Large lake (3 words)
10. Aboriginal group

Answers

Canada crossword pages 2–3

Canada word search page 4

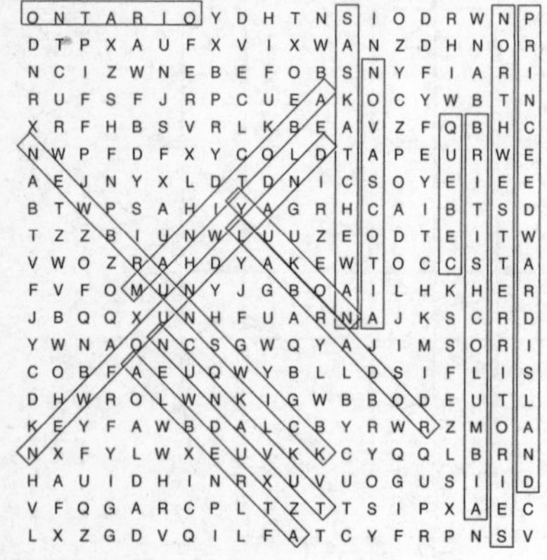

Maple Maze page 5

History Mysteries pages 6–7

1. Alexander; 2. Laura; 3. Samuel; 4. Jeanne

British Columbia crossword pages 8–9

Northern Lights page 10

Whitehorse; Yellowknife

Secret Codes pages 12–14

Sports

1. badminton; 2. soccer 3. tennis; 4. hockey; 5. racing

Languages

1. Spanish; 2. Italian; 3. Hebrew; 4. French

Canadian Riddles page 15

1. because he's alive; 2. the buck and the doe (get it, dough?); 3. halfway — after that, he's running out; 4. no! He's dead; 5. white — the house is at the north pole

Alberta crossword pages 16–17

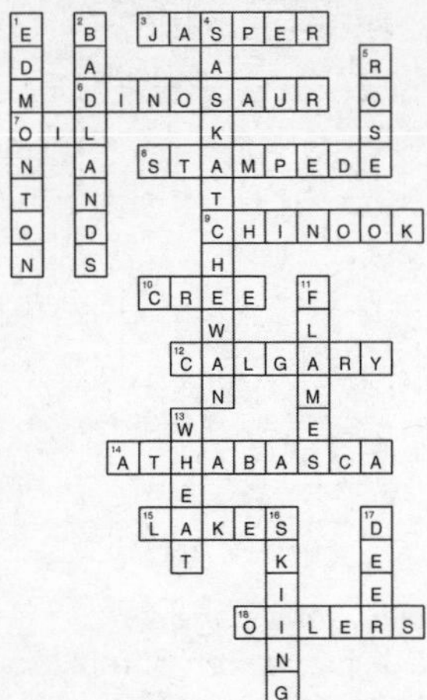

Scrambled Names page 18

1. Alexander Mackenzie; 2.Terry Fox; 3. Pierre Trudeau; 4. Edmonton; 5. Emily Carr; 6. Wayne Gretzky; 7. Louis Riel; 8. Avril Lavigne; 9. Lake Superior; 10. Robert Munsch

Hockey Maze page 19

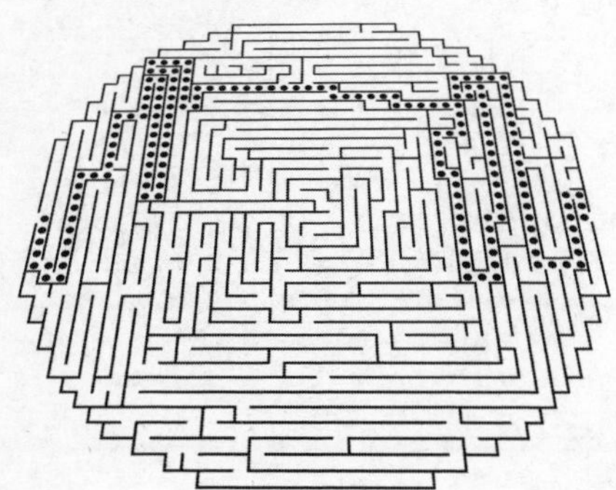

How's Your Logic? pages 20–21

1. your mother
2. The two boys go over first. One of them returns with the boat and one parent goes across alone. The second boy then returns with the boat, gets the other boy, and they go across again. One of the boys takes the boat back and waits while his other parent goes over. The other boy goes back with the boat and gets his brother, then the two boys go back across.
3. grandson
4. First he takes the chicken across. Then he takes the fox across and brings the chicken back. Then he takes the feed across and returns for the chicken.
5. three
6. his daughter
7. There was a grandmother and her daughter, who was also the young girl's mother.
8. Ask one man, "Which door would the other man tell me to take?" Then take the opposite door.
9. Jane explains: "The dot on my head is blue, because if it were red, then Thomas would know he had a blue dot on his head because Winnie raised her hand. Similarly, if my dot were red, then Winnie would know that she had a blue dot because Thomas raised his hand."

Saskatchewan crossword pages 22–23

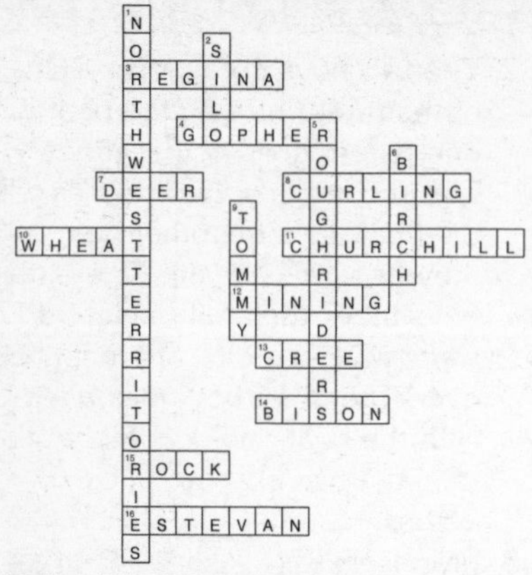

Riddle, Riddle! page 24

1. when it runs; 2. when they're in quarters; 3. the crane; 4. when it rains (reigns); 5. the buttercup; 6. noise; 7. It has two banks; 8. because they can't walk in it

A Canadian City page 25

St. John's

Beware! Wild animals! page 26

1. beaver; 2. goat; 3. bear; 4. deer; 5. moose; 6. elk; 7. skunk; 8. otter; 9. loon; 10. mink; 11. seal;

O Canada! page 27

Peace, Ottawa, square, events, seat, federal

Manitoba crossword pages 28–29

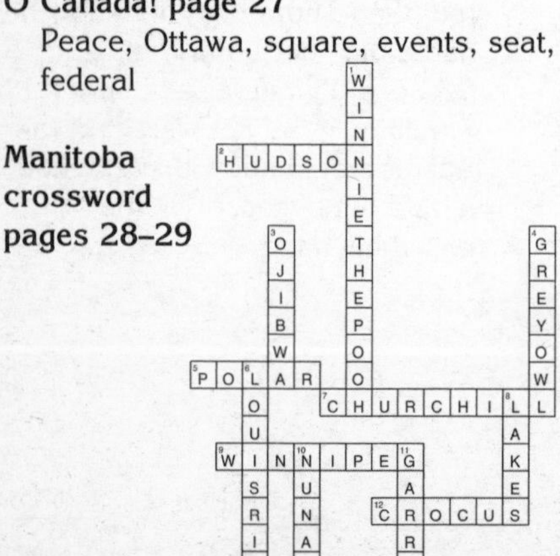

Moose Crossing page 30

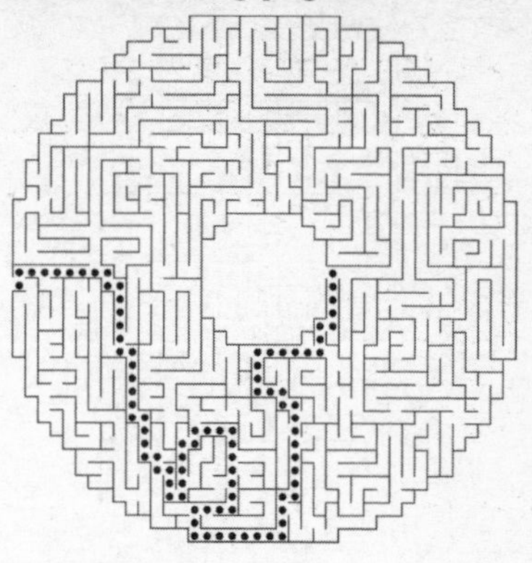

Jumbled Jobs page 31

1. dentist; 2. writer; 3. musician; 4. scientist; 5. banker; 6. actor; 7. teacher; 8. veterinarian; 9. nurse; 10. dancer; 11. photographer; 12. judge; 13. artist; 14. doctor; 15. plumber; 16. reporter; 17. pharmacist; 18. librarian

Hockey Puzzle page 32

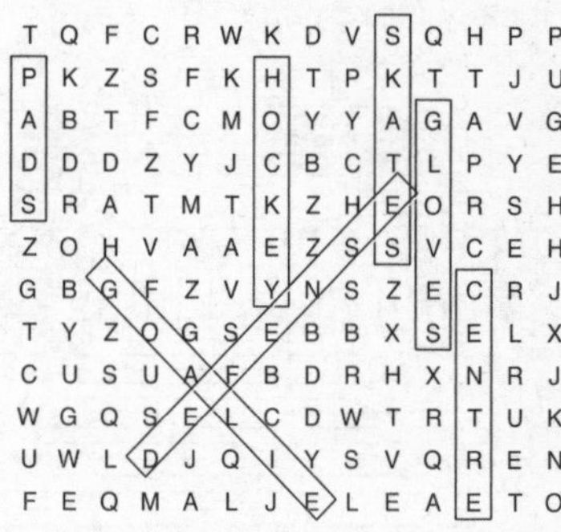

Countries page 33

1. United States; 2. United Kingdom; 3. Japan; 4. France; 5. Germany; 6. Mexico; 7. Australia; 8. South Korea; 9. Netherlands; 10. China; 11. Hong Kong; 12. Taiwan; 13. Switzerland; 14. India; 15. Italy

Ontario crossword page 34–35

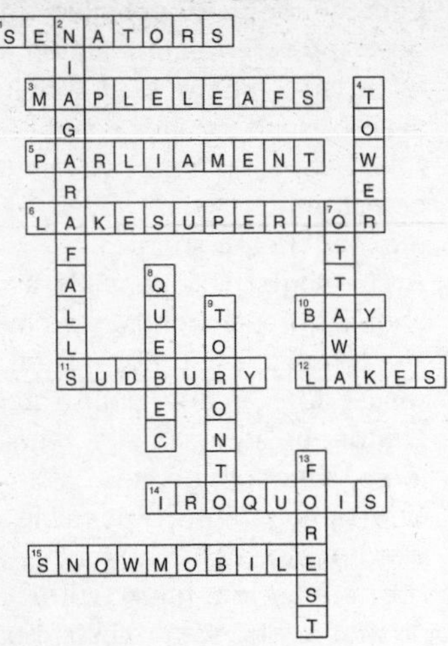

Riddle-a-City! page 36
Ottawa
And Another
Fredericton

Canadian Weather page 37
1. rain; 2. sleet; 3. tornado; 4. mist; 5. frost; 6. cloudy; 7. hurricane; 8. hail; 9. lightning; 10. snow; 11. blizzard; 12. wind; 13. fog; 14. thunder; 15. ice

Quebec crossword pages 38–39

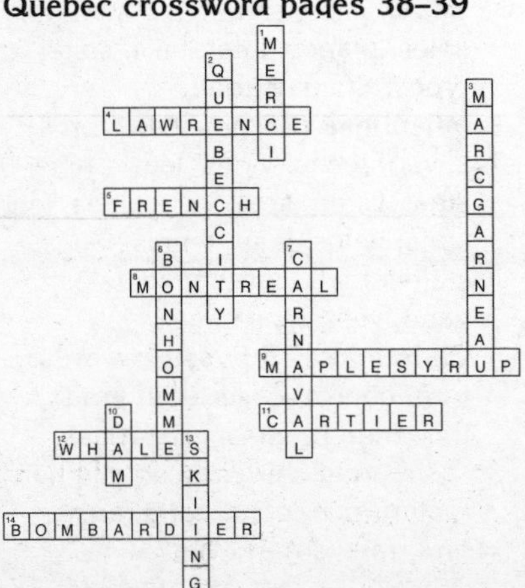

Wagon Wheel pages 40–41
1. (25 possible words): strangers, nests, rear, garage, rest, rage, tears, range, near, anger, art, gang, ears, rangers, tense, ages, gears, rag, set, sense, gets, nearer, genes, nets, range
2. (25 possible words): shoes, chose, short, toes, roses, trot, chores, hose, torch, hot, shorter, cores, sore, set, escort, scores, hoe, cot, sort, scorch, ore, rotor, tore, shores, rote
3. (25 possible words): meter, steam, meals, real, east, mere, measles, same, tease, master, rest, last, team, lame, steamer, seals, stem, sales, test, Easter, mast, easel, slam, tea, seam
4. (25 possible words): forests, roses, nests, frost, senses, tore, rest, stones, toes, store, one, foe, nor, tones, ore, sons, not, nose, snore, trot, sore, fore, forts, nonsense, fro

Hidden Words pages 42–43

Hockey
1. stick; 2. rink; 3. goal; 4. playoff; 5. scored; 6. arena

Winter
1. snow; 2. sleet; 3. ice; 4. cold; 5. frost; 6. freeze

Breakfast Foods
1. cereal; 2. egg; 3. honey; 4. toast; 5. bacon; 6. milk; 7. jam

New Brunswick crossword pages 44–45

Crack the Code pages 46–47

Cities of the World

1. London; 2. Naples; 3. Peking; 4. Lisbon; 5. Bombay; 6. Sydney

Countries of the World

1. Sweden; 2. Mexico; 3. Holland; 4. Australia; 5. Canada; 6. France; 7. Japan

Guess My Name pages 48–49

1. stockings; 2. a mirror; 3. bubble; 4. yesterday; 5. a road; 6. icicle; 7. fire; 8. a window; 9. a railroad track; 10. a chain; 11. silence; 12. a secret; 13. a stocking; 14. a river; 15. a cabbage

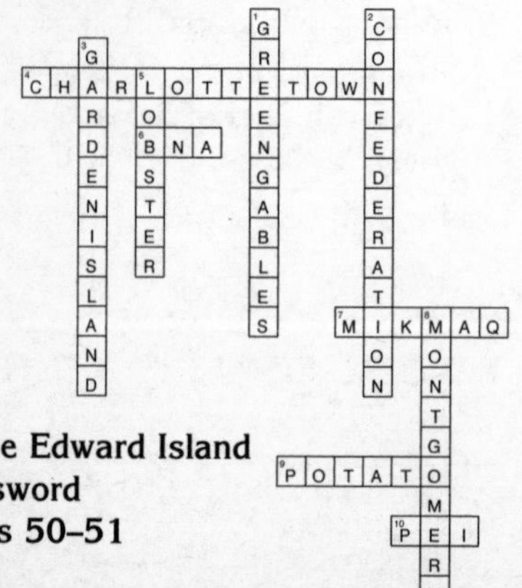

Prince Edward Island crossword pages 50–51

Hidden Words pages 52–53

Leprechauns (25 possible words): pearls, pause, reach, launch, learn, sure, share, peel, lunches, search, such, prunes, sleep, nurse, rule, chaps, spare, preaches, cares, punch, lease, sheen, phrase, cheap, sharp

Archeologist (25 possible words): choose, great, arches, starch, list, stool, holes, least, hose, steal, realist, logo, reach, goals, grates, charge, hoist, loser, silo, tears, large, salt, soil, goose

Sportsmanship (25 possible words): storm, mist, paints, sports, passion, harm, stirs, prison, prints, spin, masts, riot, hint, roast, thin, Spain, maps, torn, moth, sash, stops, train, span, pots, pianos

Ornithologist (25 possible words): lion, roost, short, grins, horns, solo, grit, logs, toots, hoist, groin, roots, loon, silo, logo, list, shirt, snoot, shot, long, song, thin, snort, lion, shoot

Personality (25 possible words): reality, stone, loans, spoil, tile, pails, tiny, seal, person, stale, Spain, piles, salt, lint, sonar, pale, spies, planes, later, tails, spite, toil, types, Stanley, trial

Valentines (25 possible words): seven, teens, vines, lease, nine, steel, listen, seal, vase, lines, lent, stale, veins, lean, tennis, lanes, stain, steal, tease, save, tales, vane, vest, tense, nest

Christmas (25 possible words): trim, charm, casts, stars, mist, this, march, cash, arts, mass, sash, arch, shirts, mast, stir, harm, match, rich, chat, carts, arms, hiss, rats, smart, mash

Destination (25 possible words): stone, test, dates, station, notes, dine, toads, instead, state, tint, neon, send, tons, dents, sand, nest, tides, stand, none, tone, dentist, neat, stain, seat, sane

Fireplace (25 possible words): ripe, pair, replace, care, fire, epic, race, fare, rail, preface, place, pear, leaf, face, flare, rice, fair, repair, reap, clear, lace, fear, flap, feel, plea

Nova Scotia crossword pages 54–55

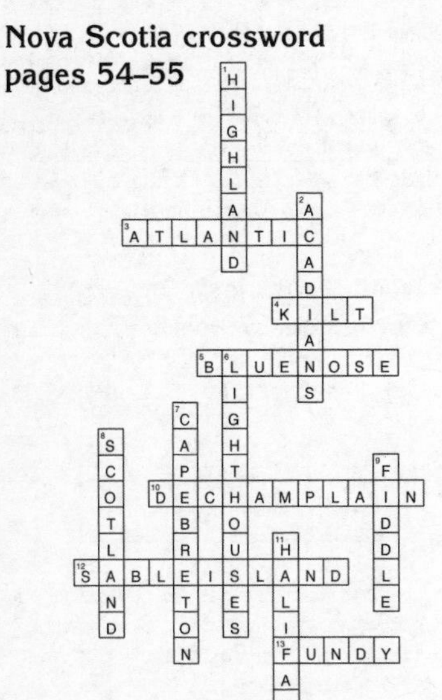

Queenly Cities page 56

Regina, Victoria

Happy Holidays page 57

1. candles; 2. Yom Kippur; 3. decorations; 4. Kwanzaa; 5. New Year; 6. Christmas; 7. Easter; 8. music; 9. Diwali; 10. presents; 11. Ramadan; 12. Thanksgiving; 13. food; 14. cards; 15. Passover; 16. Jean-Baptiste; 17. dancing; 18. prayers

Newfoundland and Labrador crossword pages 58-59

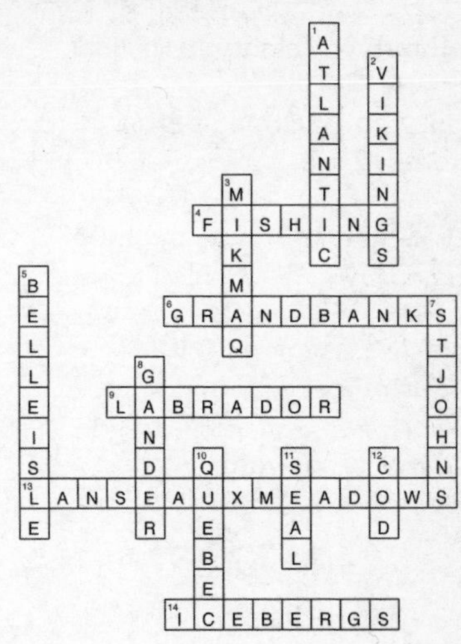

The First! page 61

John Macdonald

Yukon crossword pages 62–63

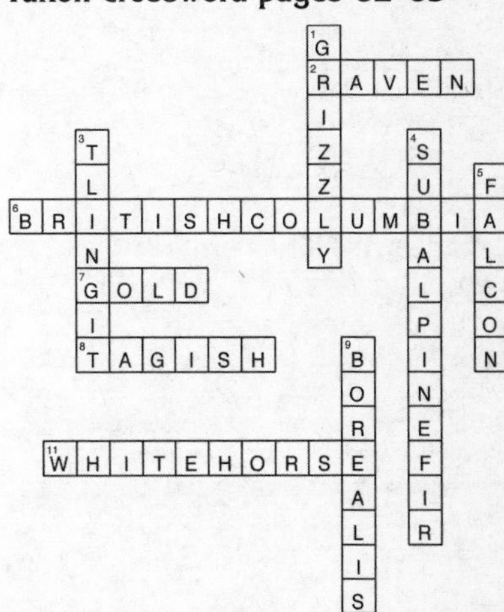

Hidden Words page 64

Numbers

1. million; 2. fourteen; 3. seventy; 4. forty; 5. eighty; 6. billion

Front and Back page 64

Toronto

Newfoundland Riddle page 65

Goose Bay

Quick'n Easy page 65

St. Lawrence

Nunavut crossword pages 66–67

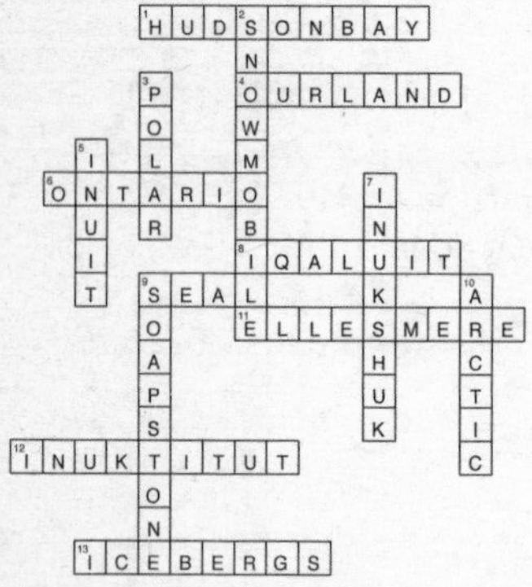

Canada's Wildlife word search page 68

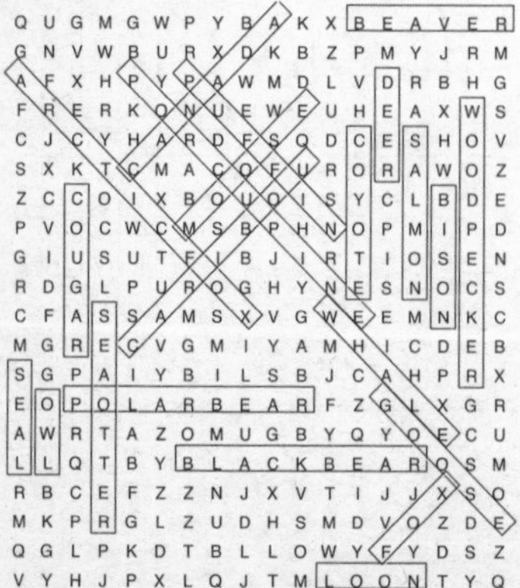

Canadian Landmarks word search page 69

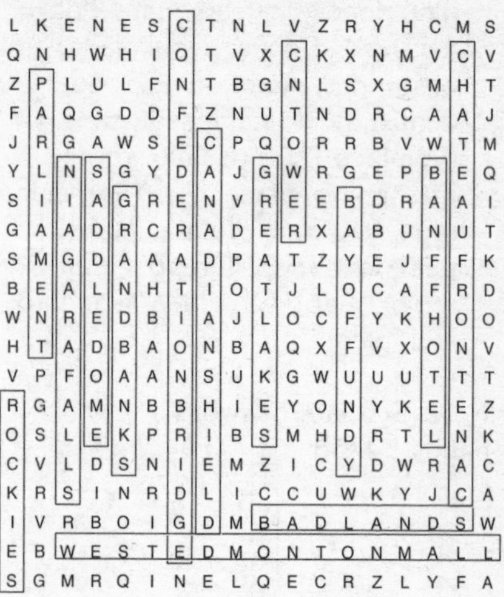

Northwest Territories crossword pages 70–71

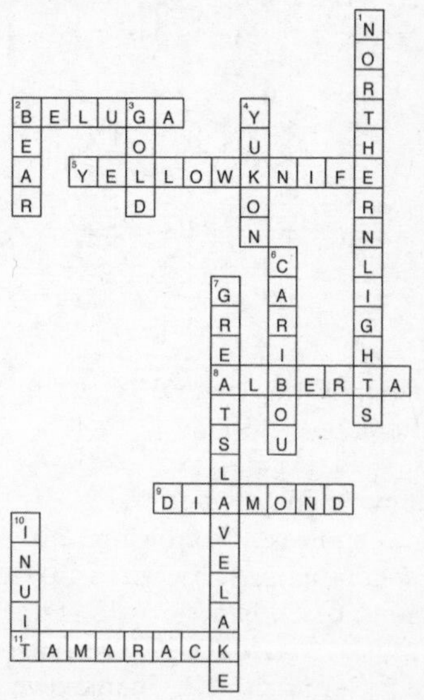